MW01296685

Contents

Introduction

Life is unfortunately rife with many ups and downs that often corrode our psychological health. Enduring memories of a negative past have the potential to mar the life we live today. Many have been afflicted by their traumatic past and still remain manacled to a toxic way of living.

Eye Movement Desensitization Reprocessing (EMDR) is a highly specialized form of therapy that focuses on dismantling and properly processing negative memories that prohibit us from reaping the unending glories life has to offer. EMDR provides a viable avenue to unshackle those manacles and engender the pursuit of a healthy, positive and happy living.

In respect to acquiring global recognition, EMDR remains in its infancy; however its revolutionary approach to therapy has been achieving groundbreaking results in the treatment of many psychological ailments. This book discusses the many facets of EMDR, including the eight phases of the therapy and plenty of self-help techniques that are safe to practice; it provides foundational information about the practice, dilating its history, definition and various structures of training provisions.

The eBook also provides an ample of information on who can benefit from this therapy, how it can benefit adults and children struggling with traumatic experiences and much more. Valuable instructions on how to search for a licensed EMDR therapist are given as well.

What is Eye Movement Desensitization and Reprocessing EMDR?

Eye Movement Desensitization and Reprocessing (EMDR) is a trauma therapy used extensively by over 40,000 therapists worldwide. It was developed by psychologist Dr. Francine Shapiro in 1987. As she walked through the park one day, she made a chance observation. She began to notice the intensity of her disturbing thoughts and feelings subside when her eyes swept back and forth. Being a student of psychology and a curious person in nature, Dr. Francine decided to investigate this for her doctoral thesis. In a special psychotherapy protocol, she discovered a way to employ rapid eye movements and realized it was very successful in alleviating chronic distress in victims with trauma.

It appears that employing rapid eye movements mitigates the anxiety linked to the trauma allowing the original event to be examined from a more detached perspective— somewhat like watching a movie of what transpires.

EMDR is a psychotherapy used to relieve plaguing symptoms such as anger, anxiety, guilt, depression, panic attack, sleep disturbance, and flashbacks that emanate from traumatic experiences. EMDR therapy has not only proven to be effective in reducing chronic symptoms produced by trauma, but also has permanent benefits.

Over one million people, to date, have benefited from EMDR therapy. This therapy uses bilateral stimulation of the brain, right/left eye movement, tactile stimulation and sound (e.g. alternating hand taps or a chime that pans back and forth from ear to ear),which repeatedly activates the opposite sides of the brain instigating the release of emotional incidents that are 'trapped' in the nervous system.

What does E.M.D.R. Represent?

→ **Eye Movement (EM).** Today, it appears that the beneficial effects are provided by an unchanging stimulation of the right and left hemispheres of the brain— Eye Movements accomplish this, as do bilateral altering taps or tones.

→ **Desensitization** designates the elimination of the emotional disturbance connected with a traumatic memory.

→ **Reprocessing** denotes the substitute of the detrimental, negative beliefs consorted with traumatic memories, with a more healthy and positive belief.

What sorts of problems does EMDR treat?

Scientific research has found EMDR to be an effective and swift mechanism for treating Post Traumatic Stress Disorder. So far, studies demonstrate great achievements using EMDR in treatment of the following conditions:

- Performance & Test Anxiety
- Dissociative Disorders
- Complicated Grief
- Accident Victims
- Eating Disorders
- Personality Disorders
- Phobias
- Trauma
- Addictions
- Sexual Abuse
- Depression
- Fears
- Anger
- Nightmares
- Injuries
- Victims of Crime
- Physical Abuse
- Chronic Pain
- Panic Attacks
- Disturbing Memories

A Typical EMDR Therapy Session

A typical EMDR session will go like this: the first process is identifying the topic or the event that will be targeted that day. This could be a continuation form the previous session, if the time ran out. The therapist will amass some information from you, as questions about the various facets of these memories will arise. For instance, determining how troubling it is for you to recall them, or how you may have "internalized" these events.

We all periodically encounter unpleasant or tormenting things in our lives. We can make sense of the incident without it influencing our senses or our relationship with the world or others. That is, we could still feel fundamentally okay even though bad things happen to us. But for certain people, these incidents become rendered into a negative belief about oneself or experience of the world. For example: *"I'm never good enough," "bad things always happen to me," "I'm ugly (unattractive)"*etc.

Once the target has been identified, the therapist walks you through various aspects of this disturbing event. These different aspects include a visual memory, negative thoughts you consort with the target, a more adaptive or positive thinking you would prefer to believe, how your body feels and any emotion that arise.

During EMDR, the therapist asks the client to revisit the disturbing event. The client evokes a visual image of the most traumatic incident. For example: *Image of the rapist's face.* The negative belief related to the trauma is identified. Example: *I'll never recover from this.*

EMDR assists in re-processing terrifying experiences and identifying more positive beliefs to supplant them with. Remember that you may not actually be convinced at the beginning of the treatment when identifying more adoptive or positive beliefs. This is perfectly normal, as you have been traumatized and find it difficult to see or believe them.

Example: *"It's over. I can move on with my life now," "I'm surrounded by loving people who care about me," "I have support and love in my life," "I did the best I could," "I'm attractive."*

The therapist will then ask you to rate (on a 1-7 scale) how genuine the positive belief feels when paired with the target.

Once the therapist obtains a baseline in terms of identifying a target and how you feel and think about it, you will be asked to look at an equipment which will move across from left-to-right continually (or vertically, if you choose to) while thinking of your target.

Your therapist will stop the equipment after a minute or two to check in with you. They will make a succinct note of where your mind wandered to (this will help the therapists obtain a sense of the kinds of connections you make in your mind, as it will also serve as a great insight that can help in understanding your target.)

The therapist, after checking in, will turn the equipment back on and tells you to proceed. Several EMDR sessions are carried out that way: initiating the equipment, processing the thoughts and feelings while the therapist employs bilateral stimulation. The bilateral stimulation lasts until the memory comes to be less painful.

During a session, intense emotion may come to the surface, for the memories and beliefs the therapy targets are very distressful. Although you may feel uncomfortable, this is a healthy and vital aspect of the process "Desensitization."

Desensitization becomes less emotionally reactive overtime when brooking these forceful emotions, while concurrently being conscious that you're in a safe area and that you're making a choice to target these memories with a safe person in the room. However, if you feel too overwhelmed, please understand you can call an end to this process at any time. Remember you are in control the whole time. You ask for the equipment to stop, as it is perfectly okay.

You will begin to notice, as EMDR session progresses, that the overwhelming feelings begin to subside when recalling parts of the chosen target, or thinking about connected memories that are unpleasant or distressful. This means your mind is commencing to heal.

During the session (or several sessions, if you and your therapist run out of time), your therapist may notice the negative thoughts and feelings recede greatly or even stop. When this occurs, the "Reprocessing" part of EMDR takes over. Your therapist will begin to remind you of the positive statements you identified before the process began. At this point, you're given the chance to revise it

(clients often change their statements to match it perfectly with the new insights they've created.)

This usually feels great when comfort and positive feelings arise to the surface and set in.

Following a session, you may feel a little drained. Scheduling EMDR during lunch hours and then going straight back to work is probably not a good idea. Select a good timing and space to relax. You may experience forceful emotions in the course of EMDR; nevertheless, the session is invariably concluded with an unwind condition.

How long does EMDR therapy take?

The time EMDR therapy consumes depends on multiple factors including the nature of the problem being treated, the client's history, and the client's capacity to brook intense level of disturbance. In some cases, one EMDR treatment session is suffice. It usually takes weeks to months; however, sometimes years of treatment are required.

Eight-Phase Treatment Approach

Phase 1: History and Treatment Planning

The first session of EMDR therapy involves the therapist taking an initial client history. The therapist asks about the problems, fears and behavior that prompted you to come into the therapy.

Phase	Purpose	Procedures
Clients history	• Obtain background information • Identify a fitting EMDR treatment • Identify processing targets from positive and negative events in client's life	• Regular history-taking questionnaires and diagnostic psychometrics • Review of criteria and resources • Questions concerning a) the events that have paved away for the pathology, (b) current triggers, and (c) future needs

This rudimentary case history allows several case management suggestions. The overall objective of EMDR is to achieve the most profound and comprehensive treatment effects possible while sustaining a stable client within a balanced social system. It is, therefore, very crucial to assess the case methodically and individually in order to identify the appropriate targets for processing.

What makes EMDR therapy different from other therapies is that you're not asked to discuss the traumatic event in detail. It is not the details about the event itself that are important; it is the emotions and physical sensations surrounding the event.

The therapist employs a variety of techniques to identify the large and "small t" traumas and the triggers that need to be processed.

Adult clients are asked to describe 10 most disturbing memories they possess from childhood, or a timeline may be used that visually charts the most salient incidents from birth to present. They may be asked to bring photos of their family of origin and different important figures, and asked to discuss them with the therapist.

The clinician may need to postpone concluding a thorough trauma history when working with a client who has a complex trauma history until the client has developed adequate affect regulation skills and resources to stay stable.

Once the therapist has developed a treatment plan for you from the basis of the initial assessment, the process of EMDR can commence.

Current situations are assessed for levels of distress, along with the influences of previous experiences. The precise difficulties and symptoms that the client has in the present are listed, and he is asked to remember the first time that something alike occurred.

Another beneficial procedure EMDR therapists give clients is a list of negative beliefs and asks them to check off the ones that "feel" like theirs. It appears that most salient beliefs can be divided into those involving: responsibility (*"I did, or am, something wrong"*), safety and choices.

Examples of Negative Beliefs

Responsibility (I am defective)

- I don't deserve love
- I am a bad person
- I am terrible
- I am worthless (inadequate)
- I am a disappointment
- I deserve to die
- I am shameful
- I am permanently damaged
- I am ugly (my body is hateful)
- I am not lovable

- I am stupid (not smart enough)

- I deserve to be miserable
- I am different (don't belong)
- I am not good enough
- I am insignificant (unimportant)
- I deserve only bad things
- I do not deserve . . .

Responsibility (I did something wrong)

- I did something wrong
- I should have known better
- I should have done something

- It's not OK to feel (show) my emotions

Safety/vulnerability

- I cannot be trusted
- I cannot trust myself
- I cannot trust my judgment
- I cannot trust anyone
- I am in danger
- I cannot protect myself
- I cannot stand up for myself
- I cannot let it out

Control/choices

- I cannot get what I want
- I am a failure (will fail)
- I am not in control
- I am powerless (helpless)
- I am weak
- I cannot stand it
- I cannot trust anyone
- I cannot succeed
- I have to be perfect (please everyone)
- I cannot do . . .

Phase 2: Preparation

Preparation is the second and one of the most important phases of Eye Movement Desensitization and Reprocessing (EMDR) therapy treatment. It is the point in which you are given the needed tools to cope, tolerate, and overcome all the inundating emotions you will most likely face during and after EMDR sessions.

Everyone has a certain memory in life that can either have a positive or a negative emotional effect on a person when recalled. What triggers those memories and the depth of the emotional surge they ensue completely depends on the traits and the kind of past an individual is dealing with. This is the phase in which the therapist labors to have the maximum knowledge on what those memories are, how and what triggers them, the extent of their effect, how their menacing the present, and how the patient can best contain them.

A traumatizing memory could never stay dormant. It actually has much semblance to that of a ticking time bomb; if they're not dismantled promptly and correctly they will blow up when time is up and destroy the one and only life you have, which is why there is a great emphasis placed on how indispensable this phase is.

The treatments of EMDR therapy can most certainly pose as a threat to your life if you are not first properly equipped. So when you commence the Second Phase (Preparation), the therapist will first give you an elaborate brief on what EMDR therapy is, how the sessions are conducted, the importance of the treatment and what you can expect during and after EMDR sessions.

Once your therapist feels you have acquired enough knowledge about EMDR and you consent to the treatment, he/she will then proceed to analyzing your mental stand. At this juncture you are prompt to develop an honest and personal relationship with the therapist, as this is the critical point where the therapist decides on whether or not you are a suitable candidate for this treatment, or what kind of treatment would have the most effect on you.

During this session there is no need to go into greater details about a traumatic or disturbing past event in life. But your therapist will border the subject matter and you will have to provide an authentic response. This close and honest interaction will build a sense of safety in you and get you prepared for EMDR memory reprocessing; when on the other hand, it will give way for the therapist to get a better insight of your mental stand.

To maintain stability before, during, and after EMDR sessions, your therapist will then teach you a variety of mastery skills that will help calm your nerves down, incite or increase your ability to access positive memories, and much more. Some of the relaxation or self-help techniques include, self-soothing, breathing techniques, and self-control techniques such as Safe Place, where you learn how to willingly restore a feeling of tranquility, safety, or courage when dealing with a certain emotional disturbance.

Preparation Phase normally takes about 1— 4 sessions. But for children and people dealing with difficult disorders, it might take longer.

Phase 3: Assessment

Assessment is the third phase of EMDR therapy treatment. It is the stage where the foundation for the memory reprocessing of specific targeted events is laid. It is used to access those memories and establish the first standard communication with them.

Your therapist will first identify the various components of the events that have traumatized you, and then he/she will lay out the base for the communication to commence.

There will be three things you will be asked to provide during the Assessment Phase sessions; one, *a specific scene or picture*; two, *a negative belief*; and three, *a positive belief*.

Specific Scene or Picture: Selecting an image or a scene that can best describe or represent the targeted event or experience is a fairly simple step, as you have already established that during your sessions on Phase One; be it a humiliating fall at school or at work; the physical abuse you faced as a child at home, or a daunting accident.

A negative belief or Negative Cognition (NC): This is when your therapist would ask you to verbalize the negative belief you have about yourself because of that experience. Of the most commonly used Negative Cognition statements are "I am worthless", "I don't deserve love", "I am a bad person", "I deserve only bad things" "I am helpless", "I am weak", "I am a failure" etc.. The negative cognition statements, however, differ when the pervading emotion from the targeted event is fear. In such instances, the terms are often related to vulnerability, such as "I cannot trust myself", "I cannot trust my judgment", "I cannot trust anyone", "I cannot protect myself", etc.

A positive belief or Positive Cognition (PC): You are then asked to voice the positive belief you would prefer to feel about yourself. This statement should reflect upon what is suitable for the present. If for instance you survived an accident and your negative belief is "I am not safe," it would be replaced by "I am safe now." Or if the targeted event revolved around an incident in which you made a mistake and feel morbidly guilty about, and your negative cognition statement is "I deserve to die" it would be altered to "I deserve a second chance."

Once the visual image, the negative and positive beliefs are distinguished, the therapist would then ask you to give an estimated rate of how much you believed your own positive cognition statement. You will be providing your answer though the 1 – 7 Validity of Cognition (VOC) scale – 1 means completely false and 7 means completely true. You will then be asked how and what you felt when the memory was in conjunction with the negative belief— fear, anger, sadness, hopelessness— and for this the therapist will also ask you to rate your emotional disturbance using the 0 – 10 Subjective Units of Disturbance (SUD) scale, in which 0 means no disturbance and 10 means complete disturbance.

Memory reprocessing of specific traumatizing events doesn't only have a stimulating effect on ones emotions, it can also ensue physical changes. So during the processing the therapist will also ask you to specify where and what exactly the physical sensations were when you thought about that traumatic event. Common sensations include tension in the stomach, headache or light headedness, and cold hands.

Phase 4: Desensitization

The Desensitization phase is more like the launching pad in EMDR therapy treatment. It is the stage in which a targeted memory is fully activated and you are asked to focus on the negative belief, disturbing emotions and sensations it will ensue.

In this phase, standard EMDR methods are used to administer the disturbing experiences. These procedures are structured to access the memories as they are currently stored, stimulate the information processing system, and observe the transfiguration of the collected information to an adaptive resolution. Ensuring that all significant information has been collected and addressed is the main objective of this procedure.

During the sessions of this phase, your therapist will ask you to focus on the targeted image and to attentively take note of the negative belief, disturbing emotions, and the bodily sensations that will follow, while you are at the same time attending to the bilateral stimulation (movement of the therapist's finger or other stimulating methods).

At the end of each set of stimulation or rapid eye movements, your therapist will ask you to give a brief report on all your reactions to the processing, including any new memories, insights, information, and behavioral shifts that might have surfaced. Depending on the gravity of your response, the therapist would either instruct you to focus on the recently revealed information or take your concentration back to the targeted image.

The changes in imagery, sensation, belief, and perspective are the most salient parts in the Desensitization Phase. But if the changes don't occur after a dual set of stimulation, then the therapist would use a Cognitive Interweave procedure and ask a question, voice a statement or suggest an action to stimulate the emergence of more information and continue the processing.

If for instance, a rape victim's processing is fixated at the sense of shame or blame, the therapist would ask, "Do you mean if your little sister had been raped it would be her fault?" When the rape victim responds by saying 'no', the therapist would then use the patient's agreement, even if it's with hesitation and ask for him/her to think about it during the next set of stimulation.

The desensitization phase continues until a patient returns to the targeted experience with a distress level or SUD scale of 0 – 1.

How the sessions in phase 4 – 6 are conducted

After phase three, the processing of trauma begins. And from phase 4 – 6 you will be guided by your therapist to recollect the images of targeted events while going through a series of rapid eye movements.

When you focus on the movement of your therapist's finger but concentrate on the targeted image internally, your attention would be split in two, which will enable you to go back to the past and experience all the components of the distressing memory while having a solid platform in the present. And this will facilitate you with the capacity to effectively process, understand, and restructure the trauma.

Phase 5 Installation

This phase aims at concentrating on and enhancing the positive belief you have identified to replace it with the original negative belief. At this point, the therapist assesses whether the desired positive belief identified in phase 3 is still applicable, or whether a new and more effective one has manifested.

It is not uncommon for a new Positive Cognitive (PC) to emerge and become favorably applicable even after the completion of processing, which clears away the confusion and brings to light more positive information.

In this phase the therapist attempts to link the desired Positive Cognition with the incident or original memory.

The procedure would take the following course.

- The therapist, recalling the incident or original memory, asks you if the PC applied earlier still fits or if you would like to alter it. Upon your selection, the therapist either goes along with the original PC or the new one.
- The therapist will ask you to recall the original memory and those words of PC. And then he/she will ask: "On a scale of 1-7 how valid does the PC feel?" 1 being completely false and 7 being completely true.
- You will then be asked to link the original issue in your mind to the PC and to practice 24EMs (Eye

Movement). The therapist will ask: "What happened?" or "What do you notice?"

- You will be asked to rate from 1-7 how true your positive statement feels when you think of the original incident.
- The above practice is repeated to link the PC to the original issue and to acquire positive changes.
- Should the Validity Of Cognition (VOC) fail to rise to 6 or 7despite the application of EMs, the therapist would approach using another method.
- The therapist would pose the questions: "What prevents it from being a 7?" and "What is it you need to learn about yourself for it to rate 7?"

After multiple EMs and the repeated or final rating of 7 for VOC, you can then move on to Body Scan.

Phase 6 Body Scan

This is the phase that focuses on detecting any residual physical sensation. You are asked to think of the targeted memory with the PC while scanning the body for any sensational changes. Once the sensation is discerned it is processed in consecutive sets until it is completely dispersed. At times, a sensation may be a clue to a rather uncovered dysfunctional information in which another memory may be awakened. If this proves to be the case then the issue is focused on and processed. On the other hand, the practice may evoke pleasing sensations. As these are memories connected to positive effects, they are greatly encouraged.

The session would follow the following course:

- You are asked to close your eyes, and then told to focus on the original memory and the Positive Cognition. Then you are ordered to repeat the words while scanning your entire body from head to toe. The therapist would ask, "Do you feel something; (if so) where?"
- EMs would be conducted as soon as the sensation is reported.
- The reported discomforts are reprocessed until they are dissipated.
- The positive sensations that arise are strengthened through EMs.
- Once you acquire a neutral or positive reaction, this phase is complete and you are ready to move on to Phase 7— that is, when you have a clean body scan devoid of any negative sensation.

Phase 7 Closure

This phase is purposed to ensure that you remain in a state of equilibrium when the session ends. It also aims at making certain that you remain this way between sessions. If you show distress this would exhibit the incompletion of the process so one of the guided imagery or self-control techniques is applied to eliminate the issue.

For instance, if you show a clear lack of positive self-worth, then it would be helpful to finish each session with positive, invigorating imagery that inspires and strengthens self-love, sense of control and sense of security.

In this phase, you are informed on what to expect between sessions. You are also provided TICES Log (Trigger, Image, Cognition, Emotion, Sensation/SUD) which are short journals that are employed to discern negative or positive experiences. As you process the trauma throughout the week, disturbing thoughts, images, or emotions may manifest. The journal is framed to help the therapist accurately assert your state.

Trigger	Image	Cognition	Emotion	Sensation
A colleague told me I looked awkward	His face	I'm ugly	Self-disgust	A knot in my stomach

In addition to the above practices, elements of the status quo that provoke disturbances are processed. They are often assumed to be second-order conditioning. For instance, if a person frequents a place and he/she experiences anxiety walking in and out, this response can produce numerous stimuli in the area that can elicit anxiety. While it is of paramount importance to address factors of the past that have laid the groundwork for the dysfunction, it is also essential to process current events that incite disturbances. Ridding the individual from the forced negative responses is significant.

To better prepare you for the displeasing surprises that life unfortunately is rife with, self- control techniques are occasionally applied. These techniques bestow a person more control over life and allows him/her to make smarter decisions.

This session will be complete when SUDs (Subjective Units of Disturbance) have gone down to 0 or 1 and when VOC is rated 7. But it will be deemed incomplete if SUDs are above 1 and VOC is less than 7.

Phase 8 Reevaluation

All the new sessions commence with a reevaluation of the progress you have made. The first thing the therapist asks is for you to focus on earlier targets that have been processed. The therapist will, with assiduity, assess your response, checking to see if the positive results have been maintained. Between sessions, the therapist will also ask about the targets that have been treated earlier, how you feel about them and if there are any disturbances that arise.

It is based on this reevaluation that the therapist decides whether you are fitted to proceed to new targets or to revisit earlier targets that require additional reprocessing.

Past, Present, and Future

EMDR often produces results faster that earlier forms of therapy; however, it should be noted that speed is a rather subordinate matter and that clients have different paces of recovery. Some clients may take weeks to complete Phase 2 (establishing feelings of trust) and some might complete the first six phases of treatment fast and reveal setbacks such as something important that needs to be reprocessed.

Each form of psychotherapy differs in its sets of procedures and theories. For instance, in cognitive and behavioral therapies, attempts are made to address the current problems of the client by trying to change their thinking or behavior in the present. On the contrary, EMDR therapy believes that the negative beliefs and emotions, such as anxiety and fear are the effect not the cause of the problem. Instead, the causes are believed to be specific memories of past events that have been wrongly stored in the brain and continue to influence the effects and perspective exhibited through behavior, improper emotions and voiced beliefs. These memories cause the past to become the present.

In EMDR, experiences are viewed as information stored in the brain in memory networks that are stimulated by present conditions. This is quite a contrast to other therapies which propose that pathologies have experiential component.

The EMDR protocols apply the past targets (past memories contributing to the problem), present (most recent triggers) and future (template, the skills the client needs to attain for the future).

EMDR aims at liberating the individual from the dysfunctional memories that carry the perspective and effects catalyzing the current pathology. This allows the client to eliminate obstructive memories allowing him/her to proceed with life unfettered with negativity.

EMDR is not complete until the past, present and future is fully dealt with.

EMDR for Children

Rapid progress is often observed on children than adults. This is perhaps because patterns and memories haven't taken root in children as in adults, that is to say that the trauma, anxiety or phobia has had less time to be anchored in children given their tender age.

EMDR has proved to be an effective treatment for traumatized children. A mixture of individual and family sessions is applied to uncover and treat the ailments of the child.

Extra precautions are required when applying EMDR on children with very complex traumas and many overlapping problems.

EMDR Benefits for Children

EMDR has helped kids with many psychological issues.

- Big traumas emanating from perpetual abuse, a death in the family or repeated surgeries.
- Anxieties, compulsive behavior, fears, depression, sleep and eating disorders.
- Minor traumas ignited by a single scary accident, a nightmare, animal nips and social problems.
- Children struggling with situations in which they feel stuck and want to change their feelings or behavior but fail to do it alone.
- Phantom limb pain (this is when pain is felt stemming from an amputated body).
- Emotional effects of all levels of abuse—physical, sexual, emotional, and social.
- Children conflicted over the thought of who loves them and don't know how to love back because they have not bonded with their parents. EMDR has been able to produce positive results on such children.
- Those traumatized by war, volcanoes, earthquakes, floods etc.

There are many ways EMDR can help children.

Spiritually: It helps recover and rejuvenate their lost and wounded souls.

Emotionally: It greatly enhances poor self-esteem of children often caused by physical or sexual abuse.

Physically: Effective in the recovery from challenges ranging from bedwetting to phantom limb pain.

Mind wise: EMDR proves especially useful for anxiety, obsessive compulsive disorder, depression, withdrawal and low performance in school caused by traumas.

Socially: Children that are anti-social, violent or difficult to deal with because of abuse or trauma are helped through this treatment.

Questions You Should Ask Before Selecting a Therapist for a Child

- Ask what the major profession of the therapist is. For instance, if he/she is a family therapist, child psycho therapist, social worker, psychiatrist, counseling psychiatrist, nurse therapist etc.
- What is the registering organization of the therapist? You can then verify this account by contacting the prominent organizations available. If you are located in the UK and Ireland, most of the therapists should be registered with the Health Care Professional

Council (HCPC) or one of these bodies: BACP, BABCP, UKCP, GMC, and NMC.

- You should find out about the extent of the experience the therapist has in working with children and adolescents.
- Ask if the therapist is 'DBS' (Disclosure and Barring Service) checked (this is an assessment that reveals whether or not the therapist has ever been convicted of an offense against a minor). In Scotland, this is known as PVG (Protecting Vulnerable Groups). The therapist must have a certificate to verify this.
- Is the therapist a member of EMDRAI, EMDR Association of UK and Ireland or EMDR Europe? Has he/she also completed the EMDR Europe accredited generic training?
- At this juncture, there are two levels of training for EMDR therapists dealing with children. Find out if the therapist has a child training Level 1 and/or Level 2, which is validated by EMDR Europe.
- Ask whether the therapist gets constant supervision form an EMDR Europe accredited consultant who has an experience in employing EMDR therapy when dealing with children and adolescents.

When is EMDR an Appropriate Option?

EMDR therapy is used to heal big to little traumas. The big traumas include horrific events like rape, combat, or the loss of a child, while the mild traumas include everyday chronic horrors, like daily negative childhood messages occasioning a girl to grow up believing she will never be good enough.

This therapy can temporarily be an intense emotional experience. It is NOT appropriate for those who are reluctant or incapable of tolerating extremely disturbing emotions. An EMDR therapist must take a methodical history to establish if and how EMDR can be employed as part of an overall treatment plan.

If you are dealing with thoughts or behavior or feelings that are causing you distress, you should perhaps consider calling for an assessment.

Diagnosis

It is highly recommended that people with the following diagnosis resort to EMDR as an option: post-traumatic stress disorder (PTSD), trauma reaction, infidelity, panic attacks, addiction, codependency, generalized anxiety, phobia, and others.

Issues

EMDR can be a valuable choice for those dealing with emotional problems that are negatively influencing their current thoughts, feelings or behavior. Emotional ailments can emanate from childhood abuse (physical, sexual, emotional and neglect), school bullying, domestic violence, being in a car accident, bearing witness to violence, being shamed by someone considered an important figure.

Addiction

The therapy can benefit those who have abandoned addictions like drugs and drinking .Being sober can have buried emotions—numbed by the addiction earlier— appear painfully. It might prove challenging to block them after that so seeking EMDR therapy would be highly beneficial.

How to Find the Right EMDR Therapist

As EMDR is a highly specialized therapy it is of paramount importance that it is conducted by a licensed mental professional who is experienced in this intricate approach. As this is a rather avant-grade approach to therapy it is highly likely that some therapists have received insufficient training for this field or are out-of-date with the latest discoveries in the therapy.

There are two prominent organizations: the EMDR International Association and the EMDR Europe. These organizations provide a list of certified and well trained therapists who have fulfilled all the necessary requirements to practice EMDR therapy.

Here are a few questions to ask a potential EMDR therapist:

- Did you receive Part 1 and Part 2 of the basic training?
- Is your training program approved by the EMDR Europe and EMDRIA?
- What is the number of patients with my particular disorder or problem you have treated?
- Can you give me your success rate?
- What is the standard EMDR you are practicing? Is it as it is (a) depicted in Dr Shapiro's text and (B) tested in research?
- Can you tell me how EMDR can help me deal with my pronounced symptoms?
- Can you also help me understand how the application of EMDR can help me live a happier and more productive life by treating the negative beliefs, memories, actions and feelings that are possibly ruining my life?

EMDR Therapy Self Help Techniques

After having a few sessions and ensuring a safe place in the course of EMDR, most clients found that they could help themselves independently. If your symptoms are severe, then it's preferable to see an experienced therapist for a course of EMDR.

Below is an outline of some EMDR techniques you could employ on your own. They are largely sourced from Francine Shapiro's excellent book.

1) A Happy Future

1) Relax and slowly breathe several times. If you find your mind wandering, take another deep breath and bring it back to the exercise.
2) Focus on a situation in the future you'd like to deal with.
3) While still in this state of mind, decide how you would like to feel, see, act and believe.
4) Evoke a safe or calm place in your mind, possibly by identifying an experience in your past where you have succeeded.
5) Now, mention a positive thought "*I can succeed*". Concentrate on the positive feelings that arise, such as confidence, strength, clarity or calm.
6) Bring yourself to focus on an image of prosperity in the future. Concentrate on the

positive feelings and emotions and assume a posture that helps you feel self-assured.

7) Play a movie in your mind nicely, dealing with the situation from beginning to end. Make it exciting, vibrant, detailed, and enjoy the positive feelings that arise.

8) Imagine a challenge set before you. Now imagine addressing it calmly and confidently.

9) End the exercise with a successful conclusion, feeling confident, well-equipped and prepared.

2) Belly Breath

To help alleviate the disturbance, inhale slowly and deeply while feeling your stomach expand. Then slowly feel your belly contract. Repeat this several times until you feel a greater sense of calm.

3) Butterfly Hug

The "Butterfly Hug" is often employed in trauma therapy. It has proved to be very successful in helping those affected by natural disasters. You can employ the below techniques to cope with ephemeral disturbance.

1) Cross your arms in front of you, with your right hand on your left shoulder and your left hand on your right then close your eyes.

2) Create a safe and calm place in your mind along with a positive word that you connect it with. Let it pervade your mind.
3) Let it sink in naturally. Don't force it.
4) When you feel safe and calm, tap your hands alternately on each shoulder slowly 4 to 6 times.
5) Take a deep breath and see how it feels.
6) Do it again one more time.
7) Open your eyes.
8) If the positive state increases, shut your eyes once more, allow yourself to feel the feelings, and bring up the word.

This butterfly hug is an excellent technique to use on children who are prone to anxiety attacks or develop overstimulation issues.

You can put the child on your shoulder and begin gently taping each side while providing them with soothing mental images or just inviting them to be composed.

This technique could also be performed by tapping your knees while sitting on a chair. The concept is that you tap on one side of the body followed by tapping on the other side of the body. This unfetters the body's anxious and panic response and permits the brain to take charge, leading to closure of the fear and stress and supplanting it with a tranquil sense of well-being.

4) Four Elements

This technique will help ground you when you're affected by past memories or when feeling dissociative.

- **Earth**

  Take a minute or two to "land" and truly live in the present. Feel the chair supporting you while putting both feet on the ground. Observe and concentrate on what you see and hear.

- **Air**

  Inhale through your nose to the count of four, hold it for two seconds, and then exhale for four seconds. You may repeat this around a dozen times, focusing on deep, slow breaths.

- **Water**

  Pay attention to your mouth and see how much saliva you have in it. Produce more by flexing your tongue and picture the taste of chocolate, lemon or your favorite food. Although your mouth often "dries" when you're anxious, this technique can switch the response and help you relax.

- **Fire**

  Think of a safe place or another resource. When you're positively thinking and remembering, concentrate on where you feel it in your body.

5) Self-Care

If you constantly feel you're "not good enough," or have reservation on whether you are unable to recover, make sure you seek for memories that permit you to feel competent daily. Recall events where you felt loved, valuable, confident and competent.

Relish in this positive moment; allow yourself to fully be immersed in the feeling. Now, pay attention to your body; notice how you breathe, stand and hold your head when you evoke the positive memories. If you feel yourself getting triggered, try altering your breath and posture back to the way you feel in the positive states.

By practicing this daily, it will be ingrained as a habit.

6) Body Changes

To move from anxiety to excitement or other positive emotional states, change your posture or facial expression.

If you're anxious about a future event, try focusing on the positive aspects of what you are about to do. Also, try to smile or change your posture by bringing your shoulders back, straightening up and lifting your chin.

7) Light stream

If you feel disturbed, focus on the distressing sensations in your body. Identify the following by asking yourself, "If it had a _____, what would it be?" Fill in the blank with each word below.

- ❖ Shape
- ❖ Size
- ❖ Color
- ❖ Texture
- ❖ Sound (high pitched or low)

What is your favorite color you associate with healing? (This color should be different from the color associated with the upsetting body sensation.)

Envisage that this favorite colored light is penetrating through the top of your head and directing itself at the shape in your body. Imagine that the source of the light is the cosmos, so the more you utilize, the more you have available. The light directs itself at the shape of the distress and passes through and pervades it, resonating and vibrating in and around it. As it does, what happens to the shape, size or color? If the upsetting body sensation is changing in a positive way, then proceed with the same technique until you feel comfortable.

When the upsetting body sensation dispels, you can allow the light to come in and gently and easily permeate your entire head. Then, allow it to move down through your neck, into your shoulders and down your arms into your hands and out of your finger tips in a soft, gentle way. Now allow it to flow through your neck and into the trunk of your body, easily and gently. Now allow it to go down your buttocks into your legs and flowing out of your feet.

8) Tap into Your Own Memory Bank

Try recalling 4-5 positive memories. Write each memory on an index card, including accounts that are meaningful and positive to you. Concentrate on the positive feelings and where you feel the positive sensation in your body as you call these real life experiences to mind. Keep this card nearby so you can easily access it whenever you desire.

Research on EMDR

EMDR is a therapeutic method that is basically at its embryo, but so far, it has produced tremendous results. Nevertheless, not all professionals are advocates of this psychological treatment, one of whom being the British writer and critic Samuel Johnson, Harvard University psychologist Richard McNally, who said *"What is effective in EMDR is not new, and what is new is not effective."*

There are many discrediting statements leveled at EMDR; however, the results of extensive studies in 1991 prompted the American Psychological Association and the International Society of Traumatic Stress Studies to approve the validity of EMDR therapy for post-traumatic stress disorder.

None the less, an expert's wavering medical opinion is always something to put in to consideration. So if you're looking to reap the benefits of EMDR therapy, then yes, picking sides can most certainly be challenging. So please do have a look at the several investigatory results of EMDR, conducted by various organizations dealing with various disorders.

EMDR and PTSD

According to the practice guideline of **American Psychiatric Practice Guidelines (2004, p.36)** *"EMDR employs techniques that may give the patient more control over the exposure experience (since EMDR is less reliant on a verbal account) and provides techniques to regulate anxiety in the apprehensive circumstance of exposure treatment. Consequently, it may prove advantageous for patients who cannot tolerate prolonged exposure as well as for patients who have difficulty verbalizing their traumatic experiences. Comparisons of EMDR with other treatments in larger samples are needed to clarify such differences. "*

Other researches reveal the efficacy of EMDR therapy when used to treat people suffering from Post-traumatic stress disorder (PTSD), especially combat veterans, who find it extremely challenging to verbalize their emotions and the details of their traumatic experiences.

'Twelve sessions of EMDR eliminated post-traumatic stress disorder in 77.7% of the multiply traumatized combat veterans studied. There was 100% retention in the EMDR condition. Effects were maintained at follow-up. This is the only randomized study to provide a full course of treatment with combat veterans. Other studies (e.g., Boudewyns/Devilly/Jensen/Pitman et al./Macklin et al.) evaluated treatment of only one or two memories, which, according to the International Society for Traumatic Stress Studies Practice Guidelines (2000), is inappropriate for multiple-trauma survivors. The VA/DoD Practice Guideline (2004) also indicates these studies (often with only two sessions) offered insufficient treatment doses for veterans.'

— **Carlson. J. Chemtob, C.M., Rusnak, K., Hedlund, N.L, & Muraoka, M.Y. (1998).**

The practice guidelines of the **Department of Veterans Affairs and Department of Defense** (in 2010) and the **International Society of Traumatic Stress Studies** (in 2009) also recommended EMDR as an effective treatment for post-traumatic stress disorder.

Then on the other hand, the meta-analysis conducted by **Davidson and Parker** (2001) and **Chemtob, C. M., Tolin, D. F., van der Kolk, B. A., & Pitman, R. K.** (2000) stated *"Overall, the studies reviewed here provide little support for the hypothesis that eye movements are*

critical to the effects of E.M.D.R. However, a final
conclusion regarding this issue is precluded by
methodological limitations of the various studies . . .
including treatment refractory subjects, questionable
adequate treatment dosage and fidelity, and limited power
due to small samples. "

Reported Drawbacks and Benefits of EMDR therapy

As in any other medical treatments, EMDR has its merits and demerits. The greatest and the most noticeable benefit of this treatment is how fast it can unravel entrenched psychological problems and give it a lifelong resolution. But as experts have pointed out, there are certain drawbacks that need further mention.

Benefits of EMDR

- Unlike other exposure or cognitive-behavior therapies, EMDR doesn't compel patients to 'talk' about distressing events of the past and their emotions in great detail. The treatment doesn't need a prolonged analysis of the trauma. This is an aspect of the treatment that has proved to be especially beneficial for combat veterans, rape victims, and ones who have experienced a life changing traumatic event.

- EMDR therapy doesn't focus on just one thing at a time; it simultaneously works on the body, mind, and emotions. And it's more or less because of this method that EMDR can easily access and root out the problems.

- As in most therapeutic treatments, reviving the trauma is also mandatory in EMDR therapy treatments. But in EMDR, the traumatic events are ephemeral. 'Cognitive reprocessing occurs simultaneously with memory recall.'

Drawbacks of EMDR

- EMDR was primarily established to treat trauma, and so its main objective is to remedy those suffering from acute stress, Post-traumatic stress disorder (PTSD,) to be specific. It is therefore highly recommended for those dealing with heart related issues, pregnant women, or other health problems, to consult their doctor before getting enrolled in this therapy.
  And as EMDR is a therapy that has everything to do with eye movements, people with eye problems are also highly advised to consult their doctor first.

- Studies have shown the efficacy of EMDR on PTSD, but not on phobias and disorders related to panic attacks.
- As stated earlier, EMDR is a fairly young therapeutic method, and so its long term proficiency has yet to be seen.

Conclusion

It is believed in EMDR that most pathology is either caused or influenced by indelible memories of certain experiences that have been wrongly stored in the brain. EMDR is about applying systematic evaluation to explore the foundations of the dysfunction and present situations worsening the condition to completely dissipate them.

Whether it is a child or an adult, one suffering from psychological ailments can greatly benefit from EMDR.

We hope this book has helped broaden your understanding of the therapy so that you or a loved one can acquire the necessary help.

Disclaimer

The purpose of this eBook is NOT to substitute for a professional advice. But it is developed to assist in the further understanding of EMDR Therapy and to help you make a well-versed decision about whether you are eligible for EMDR Therapy or not. For more details, please consult a qualified EMDR therapist.